ARRETINE AND
SAMIAN POTTERY

ARRETINE AND SAMIAN POTTERY

CATHERINE JOHNS

PUBLISHED FOR
THE TRUSTEES OF THE BRITISH MUSEUM
BY
BRITISH MUSEUM PUBLICATIONS LIMITED

ISBN 0 7141 1361 1

Reprinted with revisions, 1977

Published by British Museum Publications Ltd.,
6 Bedford Square, London WC1B 3RA

Printed in Great Britain
at the University Press, Oxford
by Vivian Ridler
Printer to the University

ACKNOWLEDGEMENTS

I SHOULD like to express my thanks to those who have helped me in the preparation of this booklet: the Keepers of the Departments of Prehistoric and Romano-British Antiquities and of Greek and Roman Antiquities, Mr. J. W. Brailsford and Mr. D. E. L. Haynes, who gave permission for the *terra sigillata* in their Departments to be described and illustrated; Mr. Donald Bailey, who helped in a number of ways, particularly in connection with material in the Greek and Roman Department; Mr. Philip Compton, who drew the map; and above all, Mr. Kenneth Painter, who read the text, and whose advice and encouragement at every stage have been invaluable.

NOTE

INSTEAD of exact dates, names of Emperors and dynasties (e.g. 'Claudian', 'Antonine') are used in the text. These terms convey the idea of dating largely on the basis of style, and are frequently used in discussing Roman pottery. For reference, the names and reigns of the Emperors of the first and second centuries A.D. are listed below.

Augustus	27 B.C.–A.D. 14
Tiberius	14–37
Gaius (Caligula)	37–41
Claudius	41–54
Nero	54–68
Galba, Otho, and Vitellius	69
Vespasian	69–79 ⎫
Titus	79–81 ⎬ Flavian
Domitian	81–95 ⎭
Nerva	95–98
Trajan	98–117
Hadrian	117–138
Antoninus Pius	138–161 ⎫ Antonine
Marcus Aurelius	161–180 ⎭

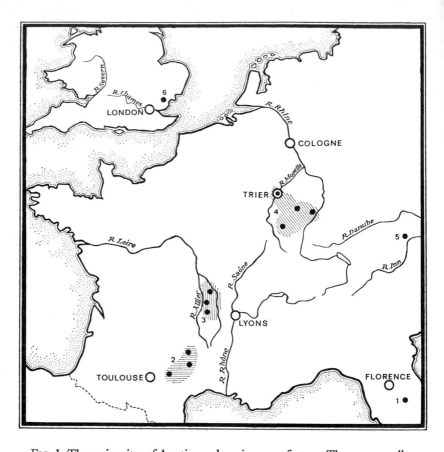

FIG. 1. The major sites of Arretine and samian manufacture. The many smaller potteries, especially in the East Gaulish area, are not shown.
○ Modern towns. ● Pottery workshops. 1. Italian: Arezzo. 2. South Gaulish: Montans, La Graufesenque, Banassac. 3. Central Gaulish: Les Martres de Veyre, Lezoux, Vichy. 4. East Gaulish: Trier, La Madeleine, Blickweiler, Rheinzabern. 5. East Gaulish: Westerndorf. 6. British: Colchester.

ARRETINE AND SAMIAN POTTERY

SAMIAN ware and its forerunner, Arretine, together form the best-known class of Roman pottery, and the museum visitor is generally attracted by their vivid colour and intricate decoration. Arretine ware has been collected and admired since the Renaissance in the same way as Greek painted pottery, and regarded as an example of the high standards of classical taste and craftsmanship. These wares are, however, as interesting to the archaeologist as to the art historian, for they can be very closely dated.

Both wares can be broadly termed 'Roman red-gloss pottery', but the names 'Arretine' and 'samian' are accepted and convenient, and will be used here. Arretine is named after Arretium, the modern Arezzo, in North Italy, which was the main centre for its manufacture. Samian, referred to on the Continent, and formerly in this country, as *terra sigillata*, was the provincial equivalent of Arretine, made in France and Germany. Both wares may be defined as Roman tableware in a fine red clay with a glossy surface, used throughout the area of Roman influence from the late first century B.C. to the early fourth A.D. The pottery was made in a variety of standard shapes, some plain, some decorated. The most frequent form of decoration consisted of figures and other motifs moulded in low relief.

The standard shapes included cups, vases, bowls, and dishes of many kinds, to be used in serving, rather than preparing, food and drink. In addition there were unusual forms for special purposes. Arretine and samian were prized above other types of pottery in their own time, and were often considered valuable enough to be mended with lead rivets when broken, where common pottery would simply have been thrown away. They have been found in all parts of the Roman Empire, and samian was one of the more common exports beyond the Imperial frontiers.

FORERUNNERS OF ARRETINE WARE

In technique, particularly in the close control of firing conditions, Greek pottery had much in common with Roman red-gloss ware,

9

but there were other, more direct antecedents in the Mediterranean area as well. For example, the glossy black Campana ware of Italy, made from the fourth to the first centuries B.C., clearly had a strong influence on Arretine plain forms. Pottery with moulded, rather than painted, decoration was inspired by relief-decorated metal vessels, and the techniques of making it, whether as complete moulded pots or as bowls decorated with applied, separately-moulded clay motifs, were well known before the days of Arretine ware. The manufacture of Arretine thus met an existing demand, and in a short time the ware had become exceedingly popular.

CENTRES OF MANUFACTURE

The manufacture of red-gloss wares was a highly-organized industry, and potteries grew up in certain areas of the Empire, with an efficient distributive network to reach all places where there was a market for their products. The siting of the potteries was determined primarily by the fact that only certain clays can be used for making true Arretine and samian ware, and it would have been uneconomic to set up a pottery too far from the region where the right type of clay was to be found.

Nevertheless distribution costs also had to be considered, and the relative importance of the various potteries at different times can be seen to be a result of the growth of the Empire during the first and second centuries A.D. The movement of the industry from Italy to South Gaul, then to Central and East Gaul, together with the establishment where possible of local manufacture in outlying districts, reflects this expansion, and was an attempt, within the limitations imposed by the siting of the raw material itself, to keep within reasonable distance of the market.

The workshops at Arezzo have already been mentioned as the major Italian ones. There were other potteries in Italy, but these were of relatively minor importance. Italian red-gloss ware flourished from the last two or three decades of the first century B.C. to the period A.D. 30–40, when it was rather abruptly superseded by South Gaulish samian. Arretine is therefore extremely rare in Britain, which was not conquered by Rome till A.D. 43.

The most important South Gaulish factories were situated at La Graufesenque, Montans, and Banassac, around Millau in southern France. Their wares replaced Arretine throughout the Empire, being exported even to Italy itself. A consignment of South Gaulish samian ware, still packed in a wooden crate, was found at Pompeii; this hoard is very useful as a chronological landmark, showing the styles of decoration popular in A.D. 79, the year in which Pompeii was destroyed.

South Gaulish ware gave way, in its turn, to samian from Central Gaul. The Central Gaulish workshops were in the valley of the Allier around Clermont-Ferrand, an area noted for pottery manufacture from pre-Roman times, and continuing as such after the production of samian had ceased. Samian was made there from some time in the first half of the first century A.D., but it was not till the second century that the wares of Les Martres de Veyre and Lezoux took over the export market from South Gaul.

The wares from the many East Gaulish potteries were popular in some areas from the early second century onwards, and much East Gaulish ware continued to be manufactured into the third century, when Central Gaulish products were no longer being exported. The term 'East Gaulish' covers a number of scattered sites; the most important as far as Britain is concerned were Trier on the Mosel and Rheinzabern on the upper Rhine. Attempts were made to establish samian manufacture in Britain, but the quality of the Colchester products was never high enough to compete seriously with imported goods. The local samian industries in Spain and North Africa were more successful, but did not export. North African wares are found elsewhere, however, after Gaulish samian died out. In the third and fourth centuries local copies of samian were made in other fabrics in many areas.

TECHNIQUES OF MANUFACTURE

The pottery centres were built up from numerous separate workshops (*officinae*), and within these, individual workmen specialized in particular aspects of samian manufacture. The making of a decorated samian bowl was carried out in a number of stages, and specialization of the potters led to speedy production.

Samian clay is very fine, and when fired in an oxydizing atmosphere (i.e., in the presence of oxygen), acquires the distinctive orange-red colour. The glossy surface is not a true glaze, but a slip, that is, a thin solution of clay in which the pot is coated before firing. It has been shown that the presence of a particular mineral (illite) causes the samian slip to fire to the characteristic smooth gloss. True glaze is usually applied to a biscuit-fired vessel, which is then re-baked, usually at a different temperature from the first firing; samian underwent only one firing, at about 1,000° C. The quality of the gloss varies a great deal on samian from different potteries and at different periods, some of the East Gaulish examples being matt-surfaced, while the better South Gaulish wares have a brilliant gloss.

To ensure that the correct oxydizing atmosphere was maintained in the kilns, it was necessary to exclude smoke; this could be done by using pipes to conduct the heat. Very rarely, samian was produced in colours other than red, but was never popular enough to justify its manufacture on a large scale. In South Gaul during the Claudian–Neronian period some marbled samian was made; the fabric is the normal pink, but the slip is yellow, marbled with streaks of red. Applied to plain vessels, this can be attractive, but on decorated vessels, for which it was occasionally used, it gives an unpleasantly cluttered effect. This ware is exceedingly rare in Britain, owing to its limited and rather early period of production.

In Central Gaul, a certain amount of black samian was produced, though, like the marbled ware, it remained a rarity. The normal samian clay was used, but one stage of the firing was carried out in a reducing atmosphere, that is, in the absence of oxygen. This process turns the slip brown or black, the core of the fabric remaining pink. The pale core, the slightly metallic sheen of the dark slip, and the fact that black samian tends to occur in somewhat unusual decorated forms (small cups and vases), all make it easily distinguishable from normal samian which has been burnt accidentally after manuafcture. The latter also turns black, but it is a matt black, and the fabric becomes hard and grey. Confusion is more likely to arise between black samian and other fine black-coated Roman wares, some of which are similar in many respects.

As mentioned above, samian and Arretine vessels were made in a wide variety of shapes; these forms were standardized, though changes occurred with time. Even the sizes of some of the more common forms were standardized to some extent. Especially in the earlier period, plain forms often had intricately shaped profiles, inspired ultimately by metal prototypes. It would have been essential to use a template in the shaping and trimming of these vessels, and it is clear that such methods were also used in making other, simpler plain forms.

The techniques of decoration fall into four main groups, incised, barbotine, applied, and relief-moulded, of which the last is the most common and most characteristic of *terra sigillata*. The incised technique was copied from glass vessels, and is sometimes known as cut-glass decoration. It generally consists of star or leaf patterns cut on to the vessel before firing, using a sharp tool of U- or V-shaped section. This form of ornament was usually applied to vases.

Barbotine, or slip-trailing, is found in its simplest form on cups and dishes with everted rims, which are counted among the plain forms. Simple leaf shapes and stems were applied to the rim using thick clay slip, the process being very like that of icing a cake. This type of decoration occurs on other types of Roman pottery and could be used to produce quite elaborate designs. The vase from Felixstowe illustrated on pl. 1 is a good example of barbotine-decorated samian, in this case combined with the applied (often called appliqué) technique.

Appliqué decoration was never very common on Arretine and Gaulish red-gloss ware, probably because it is fairly slow and difficult to make compared with the moulding of complete bowls. Single applied motifs are sometimes found on the walls of straight-sided Arretine dishes, and later, appliqué motifs were occasionally used on Central Gaulish vases. An outstanding example of Central Gaulish origin is the Cornhill vase (pl. 8*a*). The motifs, which might be human figures, animals, or leaves, were made in moulds and attached to the surface of the vase, using slip to secure them. The process is the one used in modern times on Wedgwood 'Jasper Ware', though in that case a contrasting colour of clay is used for the decoration, and the completed vessel is not slipped or glazed. Vessels like the Cornhill vase are exceptional; appliqué motifs were more usually used singly on small handled vases. In Central Gaul the post-samian workshops produced vases with three handles and three applied medallions bearing moulded relief decoration.

The low relief-moulding made by casting the whole vessel in a mould is the most typical form of ornament on samian and Arretine ware. The first items necessary for this process were the positive stamps or punches (sometimes called *poinçons*) used for impressing the decorative motifs in the mould. They were made of fired clay and making them must have been a highly specialized branch of the industry. The Arretine and Central Gaulish specimens illustrated on pl. 16 show how fine they could be; Arretine examples may sometimes have been taken, by means of a negative, from decorated silver vessels. The stamps were made with a curve in the profile which would fit the inner wall of the mould into which they were pressed. Motifs which needed to be repeated continuously all round a vessel were sometimes made on a 'roulette' stamp, a little wheel which could be rolled round the inside of the mould. As the standards in the making of samian deteriorated in the third century, the artistic standard of these stamps or punches became progressively lower, until finally the art of making them died out altogether. Some of the later East Gaulish examples are very crude indeed; where possible, the East Gaulish potters would copy figure-types by moulding them from bowls or moulds, rather than attempting to make their own. This copying led to reduction in the size of the type through the shrinkage of the clay in drying, and to severe blurring of detail, sometimes rendering the type almost unrecognizable.

The mould was a wheel-thrown bowl of fine, smooth clay, its inner profile corresponding to the desired outside profile of the final bowl, up to the upper limit of the decoration; the mould was usually provided with a flange for ease in handling and a small hole in the centre base to station it on the wheel during the forming of the pot.

While the clay of the mould was still soft, the pattern would be impressed on its inner surface by means of the stamps. Some details were added freehand with a stylus. For example, the stems and tendrils of the leaf-scrolls used on some South Gaulish ware were drawn, while the leaves and rosettes were stamped. After drying, the mould would be fired in the usual way.

The bowl was formed in the mould using soft clay, not clay in a fluid condition, as the modern slip-casting method, and the inner surface was shaped; the rim of the vessel would be drawn up above the upper edge of the mould. Because samian clay is fine and contains little filler (material, such as sand, adding to potting clay to reduce its plasticity), it shrinks considerably on drying. This would facilitate the removal of the bowl from the mould. Even so, it is not uncommon to see decorative details which have been blurred during this process. After removal, the bowl was finished by trimming and turning the rim and by forming the foot-ring; on forms with a low foot-ring, this was a case of turning away surplus clay, but bowls with a high foot-ring had extra clay added and shaped at this stage. Finally the dry bowl was dipped in the prepared slip, and after further drying would be ready for the kiln.

It is easy to see how different aspects of the work could have been carried out by different workmen; the making of stamps and of moulds, and the making and finishing of bowls could be separate specializations, and one may well imagine that jobs like the mixing and preparation of clay and slip and the supervision of the kilns would have been entrusted to individuals as full-time occupations.

POTTERS' STAMPS

Linked with this feature of the organization is the matter of the potters' name-stamps and their significance. On many plain vessels, a name is stamped, in raised letters on a sunken background, in the bottom of the vessel. The name is often accompanied by the letters F, FE, or FEC (for FECIT, 'made it'), or M or MA (for MANU, 'by the hand of'). These are stamps applied by the man who actually fashioned the bowl, and were probably used primarily as a check on the output of individual workers, which would have been necessary where several potters were making vessels of the same shape. This interpretation is borne out by the fact that the stamps occur frequently on common forms and seldom on more unusual ones. The pots of somewhat less popular type may well have been produced by only one craftsman in the workshop, and there would be no need for a distinguishing mark on them, as his output would be self-evident. Sometimes, especially in the later periods and in East Gaul, the stamps are unintelligible, and are not formed of real letters. Sometimes, too, small rosettes or other pictorial motifs were used in the place of name-stamps. These marks would have been adequate for identifying a particular man's work.

The stamps found on the most common shape of decorated bowl from the South Gaulish factories are of this type; they are bowl-makers' or finishers' stamps, and thus any attempt to link the names with the style of decoration, determined by the mould-maker, is usually futile. It can sometimes be shown that one and the same person was responsible for both mould and bowl, but this is not common.

The mould-maker's name appears from time to time on completed pots. When it does, it is most often in the form of a signature rather than a stamp, having been written with a stylus in the mould, generally beneath the decorated area, but sometimes amongst the decoration. The letters then appear as raised ridges on the finished bowl, and the whole is of course a mirror image of the original signature. When the signature is on the plain area beneath the decoration, it is often partially obscured during the finishing of the foot-ring; in this position, the name was probably not intended to appear on the finished product at all, but was written in the mould merely to identify it as the potter's property. When these names do occur, and can be deciphered, they are a real guide when considering styles of decoration. While the large workshops or *officinae* would no doubt have employed their own mould-makers, it is possible that there may have been free-lance potters who sold moulds. Some of these details are not yet clear.

The type of stamp most often found on decorated vessels is the large factory- or advertisement-stamp. The name appears in large,

PLATE I

M. 2366. A vase of Déchelette form 72 in Central Gaulish fabric of the Antonine period. The combination of barbotine and applied technique invites comparison with the Cornhill vase (pl. 8*a*), but this piece makes greater use of the slip-trailing technique, and is artistically more satisfying. It has much in common with barbotine-decorated colour-coated wares made both in Britain and on the Continent in the second and third centuries. Height 20·8 cm; max. diameter 19 cm.   81·6–26·9   Felixstowe, Suffolk

PLATE II

M. 124. Marbled samian; the form is Hofheim 8, and the cup is stamped by the potter Castus of La Grau-fesenque, who worked in the Neronian period. Diameter 10·9 cm, height 5·3 cm.　　Bordighera, Italy

(*Greek & Roman Antiquities*)

prominent letters among the decoration, often with the letters OF, signifying OFFICINA. The names were intended to be seen, and sometimes the stamps were made to read from right to left, so that the name would read correctly on the bowl. The bowls by Paternus and Cinnamus (pls. 8*b* and 10*b*) illustrate this kind of stamp. Advertisement stamps were most common on Central and East Gaulish wares of the latter half of the second century, but may also be found on some South Gaulish bowls.

It is not uncommon to find decorated bowls bearing the large advertisement stamps of a potter (or rather, firm) such as Cinnamus of Lezoux in the decoration, with the cursive mould-maker's signature beneath or a bowl-finisher's stamp on the plain rim, giving different names. This emphasizes the different meanings of the types of stamp. In the past, the potter's stamp has very often been regarded as the name of the man who 'made the bowl', but when dealing with the samian industry, this is an oversimplification.

Inscriptions other than name-stamps sometimes occur on samian, generally convivial exhortations such as BIBE ('drink!'). These are not common. Graffiti (inscriptions or other symbols scratched on a bowl after firing) are often found, and have nothing to do with the manufacture of the pottery. They frequently give the owner's name. Occasionally a longer text will be found (pl. 12*b*).

DATING: FORMS

The archaeological value of any material lies not in its appearance and in the degree of technical skill required to make it, but in the contribution it can make to one's knowledge of a culture, and this involves, amongst other things, its usefulness for dating. It will be seen that the existence of potters' names is important, as vessels bearing the same stamp are likely to have been made within the working life of the potter. Where different styles of decoration can be distinguished, an even more detailed picture builds up. But before moving on to a discussion of the chronological significance of decoration and fabric, the importance for dating of the actual shape of the pots may be considered.

All the common forms of *terra sigillata*, and many of the rare ones, have been classified and numbered by various authorities. The first detailed study was made by a German archaeologist, Hans Dragendorff, in 1895; he dealt with both Arretine and samian, and his table of fifty-five forms remains the standard classification. His numbers are referred to with the prefix 'Dr.' or 'Drag.'. Since then, other writers have added to Dragendorff's list of forms, or put forward different tables of their own, which overlap with Dragendorff. This can be a little complicated, as one shape may sometimes be referred to by two or three different numbers. Furthermore, practice varies in different countries, and the type which in England is called 'Ritterling 8', giving the author's name, is called in Germany 'Hofheim 8', quoting the name of the site. However, for most purposes it is necessary to know only a few of the commoner forms; some of the more important ones are illustrated on Fig. 2. Figure-types on decorated samian have also been classified and numbered. A number with the prefix 'O.' refers to Felix Oswald's index of figure-types.

Changes in fashion and the increasing demand for red-gloss wares led to changes in the shapes of vessels, changes which can be useful in placing them within their chronological context. Arretine and early South Gaulish wares tended towards angular, clear-cut shapes in plain ware, often derived from metal prototypes; forms such as Dr. 16 and 15/17 had finely detailed profiles which would have required care to make. Shapes very like these were made in the fine native Gallo-Belgic ware on the Continent. Some Arretine forms, such as the cup, form Haltern 8, survived only through the very first period of manufacture in South Gaul, while the Dr. 15/17 referred to above continued to the Neronian period and later. At the other end of the scale, certain forms were not made until the late second century, and are not to be found in South Gaulish or Arretine ware at all. In general, the shapes become coarser and more rounded, and were quicker and easier to make. An example of a late form is the flanged hemispherical bowl Dr. 38, common in Central and East Gaul in the late second century, and much copied in other fabrics. The samian mortarium with a lion-head spout (pl. 11*b*) also emerged late, and can still be found, though in appallingly bad fabric, on some fourth-century German sites. The long-surviving forms also changed

18

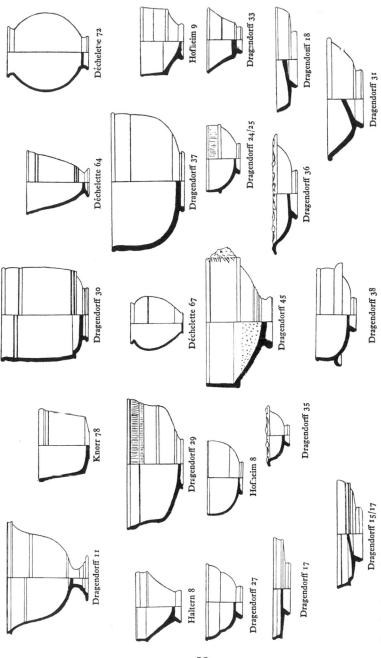

Déchelette 72

Hofheim 9

Dragendorff 33

Dragendorff 18

Dragendorff 31

Déchelette 64

Dragendorff 37

Dragendorff 24/25

Dragendorff 36

Dragendorff 30

Déchelette 67

Dragendorff 45

Dragendorff 38

Knorr 78

Dragendorff 29

Hofheim 8

Dragendorff 35

Dragendorff 11

Haltern 8

Dragendorff 27

Dragendorff 17

Dragendorff 15/17

FIG 2. Some of the more common Arretine and sarrian forms. Dragendorff 11, 29, 30, and 37, Déchelette 64, 67, and 72, and Knorr 78, are decorated forms.

19

with the years, and the little cup, Dr. 27, which, including its Arretine prototype, was made from the early first to the early third century A.D., can quite well be dated on grounds of shape and size even before fabric and potters' marks are taken into account.

Decorated forms also reflected some change in fashion; typical of Italian *sigillata* were small beakers and the elegant pedestalled bowl (crater), Dr. 11. The latter continued to be made in South Gaul up to about the middle of the first century, but it was never common there, and died out after that date. The carinated bowl, Dr. 29, is the typical South Gaulish decorated form, and occurred in Italy only as a late copy of the provincial product (pl. 3*b*). In the Flavian period, the Dr. 29 began to be replaced by the simpler hemispherical bowl, Dr. 37, and apart from a few rare early-second-century examples from Central and East Gaul, Dr. 29 ceased to be made. Certain unusual decorated forms were made only in particular areas and for short periods, e.g. Déch. 64 and 66, which are typical of the workshop of Libertus of Lezoux in the Trajanic period. The straight-sided cylindrical vase, Dr. 30, was made from the earliest South Gaulish period till the times of some of the most debased East Gaulish wares, though its appearance changed in some details.

DATING: FABRIC AND DECORATION

The change in the appearance and feel of the clay is important when dealing with small, featureless sherds from plain vessels: the fabric is in these cases the only basis for attributing the vessel to a particular centre of manufacture, and for dating it. Colour, hardness, density, and quality of the gloss all come into the question, and while the difference between one of the best products of South Gaul and one of the worst of East Gaul is easily distinguished, there are some fabrics from different areas which are not at all easy to tell apart even for the experienced hand and eye.

On decorated bowls, the style of the ornament is a further aid to identification; it is often possible to assign a relief-decorated piece to a particular workshop or group of potters. The changes and development of fabric and styles of decoration will be dealt with together.

1. *Arretine*

Arretine can nearly always bo diotinguiched from provincial products; the fabric is fairly pale and light in weight and the vessels generally quite thin-walled. The gloss is often of excellent quality in smoothness and evenness, but is never very shiny, and sometimes definitely matt. It tends to a light colour, orange rather than red. Some late, inferior Italian wares are a dull darkish red, but these were not important for export as they belong to the period of South Gaul's ascendancy.

The designs on decorated Arretine tend to be elegant and restrained. The small straight-sided beakers very often have patterns formed mainly of foliage and rosettes or flower-like motifs. Details like theatrical masks are sometimes added, as well as decorative borders. The wine-craters, Dr. 11, are usually ornamented with human figures. The designs are well balanced and not crowded, and there is commonly a theme (dancers, banquet scenes, illustration of a myth, and so on); the bowl shown on pl. 1*a* is decorated with figures depicting the Seasons. The modelling of the figures is often of a very high standard indeed.

The upper border of the decoration on the wine-craters is usually formed by the ovolo, or egg-and-tongue ornament. This motif, which has a long history as an architectural ornament, continues to be characteristic of all red-gloss wares till the latest times, and even small differences in the shape of an ovolo can be a guide in assigning a piece to a potter or workshop.

2. *South Gaulish ware*

The earliest products of South Gaul are as rare in Britain as Arretine, for they, too, pre-date the Roman conquest. The factories at Montans started work before those at La Graufesenque, some time in the reign of Tiberius. These first South Gaulish bowls are much darker than Arretine, but also somewhat harder and denser. The slip is fairly dull and brownish-red in colour. Plain forms were fairly close copies of Arretine, but the characteristic decorated form was Dr. 29, with its double frieze of decoration divided by a moulding, and the rim ornamented with 'rouletting', a kind of over-all stippling. These early bowls, though technically sometimes a little uncertain, are very beautiful in form and decoration. The latter consists typically of naturalistic leaf-scrolls. The Dr. 11 form was also made, and it is interesting that it, too, is normally decorated with leafy patterns, though in the Arretine examples advantage was taken of the larger surface of this form to use human figure-types. The South Gaulish stamp-makers may have been wise to confine themselves to the leaves and rosettes which they modelled so well, since they evidently did not share the Italian talent for representing human figures.

Early in the reign of Claudius, that is, about the time of the Roman invasion of Britain, the wares of South Gaul entered their most illustrious phase, and took over the export market from Italy. At this stage the potters achieved complete control over the technical processes, while retaining to a great extent the simplicity of decoration of the preceding period. The clay is fine, dense, and orange-pink, and the slip often of mirror-like brilliance and a bright orange-red colour. The moulding remains sharp and clear. Small animal figure-types begin to appear in the designs at this time, birds, hounds, and hares, which, however, remain subordinate to the 'leaf-scroll' theme. Plain vessels stayed close to Arretine in form, thin-walled and neatly finished.

A few pots of this period are found on the earlier British sites (London and Colchester, for example), and they are abundant on the Continent.

Increasing production throughout the Claudian and Neronian periods led to slight changes, both in the ware and in the style of decoration. On the whole, the standard remained high, but the ware started to darken in colour, the gloss to dull, and the moulding of decorated ware tended to be less sharp; possibly the increasing demands made it necessary to go on using moulds after they had lost their initial clarity. The range of motifs widened considerably and large human and animal figures were introduced, while the scroll designs of the Dr. 29 acquired medallions and panels. From the very beginning, South Gaulish figure-stamps were clumsy and provincial-looking, forming a sad contrast to the beautiful plant forms of the earlier decoration.

From the time of the Emperor Vespasian (the Flavian period) a complete change came over South Gaulish samian. It is the wares of this period which are found in large quantities on first-century British sites, and regarded as typical of South Gaul. During this phase, the Dr. 29 bowl was replaced by the simpler Dr. 37, there were many changes in the plain forms, and the appearance of the clay altered. Flavian South Gaulish ware has a soft, dusty-pink fabric, characteristically carrying tiny cream-coloured flecks, and the gloss, varying from a soft, slightly 'soapy' shine (not the clear brilliance of Claudian ware) to matt, is coarser in texture and of a darkish red, without either brown or orange tint. Moulds were made of coarser clay, a fact which is evident in comparing the rough appearance of decorated ware with the smoother plain vessels.

Designs with human and animal figure-types were the rule in this period. The Dr. 37 bowl was often decorated with many panels divided from each other by zigzag lines, the panels each containing figures and other motifs; normally there was no connection between the figures and no over-all theme in the design. Sometimes the 'free-style' bowl appears, showing either animals hunting each other, or being hunted by humans, the design not being divided up in panels. This style remained popular throughout the second century. In South Gaul in the Neronian–Flavian period, it was best represented in the work of Germanus, whose designs had some originality, and whose figure-types were well above the generally rather low standard. Germanus was much copied.

By the beginning of the second century, South Gaulish ware had become very poor and unattractive, and the Central Gaulish factories, in production since at least Claudian times, took over the supply of red-gloss pottery to most of the Empire. Some East Gaulish potteries also started at about this time. Production continued in South Gaul till probably the second half of the second century, with a primarily local distribution. The workshops at Banassac turned out much of this late ware, which is coarse and ugly. The date is indicated by the fact that these wares sometimes copy forms and decorative motifs typical of Antonine Central

Gaulish ware. The progressively less skilful copying of the types reduced them in the end almost to caricatures.

3. *Central Gaulish ware*

Although there were earlier products of Central Gaul, which are of great interest to the specialist, the pottery made at Lezoux and Les Martres de Veyre around the turn of the first and second centuries is the first to be of importance outside its own region. The Trajanic Central Gaulish products seem to have been made in a few workshops only, but were turned out in large quantities and are common on British sites. The ware is not at all unlike that of the best South Gaulish period, seventy years previously; the styles of decoration are, however, totally different. The ware is hard, dense, and orange-pink, and the orange gloss is often very lustrous. Decorated vessels are normally not quite as smooth as Claudian South Gaulish examples, presumably owing to the use of somewhat coarser clay for the moulds. The walls of the vessels are thicker, though not as thick as the immediately preceding late South Gaulish ware.

The decoration of the bowls of Dr. 30 and 37 included a wide variety of human and animal figure-types, together with many small decorative details (rosettes, cups, shields, masks, and so on), which were used to fill up spaces in the crowded, but lively patterns. It is interesting to note that the figures owe little or nothing to South Gaul; the human types are well modelled, and though not up to the Arretine standard, they are distinctly classical in appearance. The freestyle by the potter known as the 'Potter of the Rosette' (pl. 7*b*) illustrates the attractiveness of these types, in this case animal rather than human.

By about A.D. 120, the industry in Central Gaul was expanding, and a gradual change was taking place in fabric and ornamentation. Vessels tended to become larger and thicker, and the gloss duller. In the Antonine period the bowls are much coarser in appearance, the moulds leaving a pitted surface on the background area of the decoration. The ware is orange, with some tendency towards a brownish tone in the products of certain workshops. It must be emphasized, however, that though this ware is not especially beautiful, it continued to be competently made. The most important factory throughout the second half of the second century was the firm of Cinnamus. Most of the designs from his workshop are based on somewhat uninspired panels and medallions, but he had one mould-maker who specialized in large leaf-scrolls, formed of naturalistic sycamore leaves, and these can be quite attractive. A large number of the figure-types in use at Lezoux during this period had originated in the workshop of Libertus, which flourished in Trajanic and early Hadrianic times. Libertus was an innovator who experimented with unusual forms and fabrics—he made black samian—but his normal ware is often very untidily made, though imaginative in design. The style of the other Trajanic Central Gaulish potters had less influence, far fewer of their figure-types and details being handed on than those of Libertus.

Having supplied samian to most of the Empire for a hundred years, the workshops of Central Gaul appear to have ceased exporting rather suddenly at the end of the second century, perhaps owing to the political upheavals of the time. Inferior samian continued to be made in the area, together with other types of pottery, in the third century.

4. East Gaulish wares

One cannot speak of a particular fabric or style of ornament on East Gaulish *terra sigillata*, as the term covers pottery from a number of different areas, and of widely differing style. Most of the East Gaulish factories are of little importance as sources of supply for the British market. A few of the products of Rheinzabern and Trier are found here in late second-century contexts, and of the earlier wares, pottery from the La Madeleine workshops very occasionally occurs.

The earliest East Gaulish samian potteries, such as the workshops of Satto and Saturninus at Chémery, worked in the South Gaulish tradition as far as figure-types and designs were concerned. Of those setting up in the early second century, La Madeleine copied from Central Gaulish designs, while Trier had a distinctive style of its own from the start. Early Trier samian is well made, and attractive figure-types and details are used in balanced and uncluttered schemes of decoration. The standard declined steadily however, till, in the late second and third centuries, the moulded ware had become very crude and primitive. The better period of Trier manufacture is not represented in this country; a few of the late bowls only are found.

Rheinzabern ware at first showed a strong Central Gaulish influence. Designs of the Hadrianic and early Antonine period use copies of Central Gaulish figure-types in panels and medallions closely modelled on the designs produced at Lezoux. The ware is generally darker in colour than Central Gaulish. While worn-out or broken stamps at Trier seem to have been replaced by ever cruder copies, the stock of types at Rheinzabern simply diminished, so that by the late second and early third century, whole bowls may be decorated with one rosette, one leaf, and an ovolo, repeated often enough to fill the available space. Finally, diagonal lines were used, scratched in the mould with a stylus; there is a very interesting late Rheinzabern bowl in which the moulded decoration has descended to this level, but the plain rim-band of the vessel has been drawn up to a considerable height and decorated with a hound in the barbotine technique.

Plain samian, and samian decorated with barbotine or incised patterns continued to be quite attractive and competently made after the making of moulded ware had become virtually a lost art. Late East Gaulish wares were not made in quite the standard forms of earlier periods, though some, including the flanged bowl, Dr. 38, and the mortarium, Dr. 45, continued true to type. Vases and beakers were often of the same shapes as pots in colour-coated wares, and occasionally have patterns or inscriptions applied in white or yellow slip.

A point of some interest which is best illustrated with reference to East Gaulish factories concerns the migration of potters from one area to another. For example, the potter Austrus, known to have worked at Lezoux in the mid second century, later moved to Blickweiler in the East Gaulish region, so that stylistically some of the samian from the latter centre is indistinguishable from Lezoux ware by the same potter. In the same way, a small workshop was set up at Sinzig on the Rhine by a potter or potters from Trier. It seems to have been in production for a very short period, and only an expert can tell Sinzig ware from Trier products of about the same date.

LATER DEVELOPMENTS

The dividing line between some late samian and samian copies and derivatives is rather fine. A good case in point is the stamped samian, known in this country and in France by the somewhat misleading name 'Argonne ware', and in Germany as *Rädchensigillata*. The ware usually resembles late East Gaulish samian, but is variable in colour, sometimes a dark red and at other times quite a light yellow-orange. The characteristic form is the Dr. 37 bowl, usually made fairly small and thick-walled, and decorated with rows of impressed stamps bearing geometric patterns of crosses, dots, and lines. Occasionally a single ovolo motif is found among these, underlining the connection with decorated samian. *Rädchensigillata* is found on fourth-century sites, and is rare in Britain.

Glossy red pottery bearing a resemblance to plain samian, and obviously inspired by it, continued to be manufactured in the Mediterranean area in the fourth and fifth centuries, and was successful enough to be widely exported. These late Roman wares appear to have been made in both the European and African countries surrounding the Mediterranean, and have been found on a few British sites, showing that trade connections still survived in spite of the changed conditions in the Empire. The huge scale of production and highly-organized system of exporting which had characterized the samian industry in its heyday, the first and second centuries A.D., had, however, become things of the past.

BIBLIOGRAPHY

THE literature on Roman red-gloss wares is very extensive, but most of it is of interest only to the professional archaeologist or the specialist in Roman ceramics. A brief selection of the basic works is given below.

GENERAL

CHARLESTON, R. J., *Roman Pottery*.
A non-specialist book, very well illustrated, which deals briefly with red-gloss wares in the context of Roman ceramics in general.

DÉCHELETTE, J., *Les Vases céramiques ornés de la Gaule romaine* (Paris, 1904).
One of the most important early works on samian, including a catalogue of figure-types. The text deals mainly with Central Gaulish material.

DRAGENDORFF, H., 'Terra sigillata. Ein Beitrag zur Geschichte der griechischen und römischen Keramik', *Bonner Jahrbuch*, 96 (1895).
The first systematic numbering of Arretine and samian forms, still in use.

OSWALD, F., and PRYCE, T. D., *An introduction to the study of terra sigillata* (London, 1920; Gregg Press reprint, 1965).
This work remains the standard textbook; it is very detailed, and the type-tables in particular are valuable, collating material from several different sources. The 1965 edition is brought up to date with a preface by Dr. Grace Simpson.

OSWALD, F., *Index of potters' stamps on terra sigillata, 'samian ware'* (Margidunum, 1931; Gregg Press reprint, 1964).

OSWALD, F., *Index of figure-types on terra sigillata, 'samian ware'* (Liverpool, 1936–7; Gregg Press reprint, 1964).

WALTERS, H. B., *Catalogue of the Roman pottery in the Departments of Antiquities, British Museum* (London, 1908).
This catalogue, though very useful, must be used with care, as it antedates most of the major works on the subject, and there are some mistaken attributions, especially regarding East Gaulish ware.

ARRETINE

DRAGENDORFF, H., and WATZINGER, C., *Arretinische Reliefkeramik* (Reutlingen, 1948).

28

LOESCHCKE, S., 'Keramische Funde in Haltern', *Mitteilungen der Alter-tumskommission für Westfalen*, v (Münster, 1909).
This report contains a type-numbering of Arretine which fills some gaps in Dragendorff's classification.

SOUTH GAULISH

HERMET, F., *La Graufesenque* (Paris, 1934).
A basic study, but not an easy book to use.

KNORR, R., *Töpfer und Fabriken verzierter Terra-sigillata des ersten Jahr-hunderts* (Stuttgart, 1919).

KNORR, R., *Terra-Sigillata-Gefässe des ersten Jahrhunderts mit Töpfer-namen* (Stuttgart, 1952).
These books are two of the most important of Knorr's many works on samian.

RITTERLING, E., 'Das frührömische Lager bei Hofheim im Taunus', *Annalen des Vereins für Nassauische Altertumskunde*, xl (Wiesbaden, 1913).
Like Loeschcke's *Haltern*, a particularly important excavation report with numbered types.

OXÉ, A., 'La Graufesenque', *Bonner Jahrbücher*, 140–1 (1936), p. 325.
This article is basically a review of Hermet's book, but it is of great importance in itself.

CENTRAL GAULISH

STANFIELD, J. A., and SIMPSON, GRACE, *Central Gaulish Potters* (London, 1958).
A detailed analysis of the decorative styles of the potters of this area.

EAST GAULISH

FÖLZER, E., *Die Bilderschüsseln der ostgallischen Sigillata-Manufakturen* (Bonn, 1913).
Material from Trier, Lavoye, La Madeleine, etc. Now somewhat out of date, and with poor illustrations.

KNORR, R., and SPRATER, F., *Die westpfälzischen Sigillatatöpfereien von Blickweiler und Eschweilerhof* (Speier, 1927).

RICKEN, H., *Die Bilderschüsseln der römischen Töpfer von Rheinzabern*: Tafeln (Ludowici, Katalog VI) (Darmstadt, 1942).

RICKEN, H., and FISCHER, CHARLOTTE, *Die Bilderschüsseln der römischen Töpfer von Rheinzabern*: Text (Bonn, 1963).
These two works deal comprehensively with decorated Rheinzabern ware. The earlier reports on Ludowici's excavations at Rheinzabern are also important.

BRITISH

HULL, M. R., *The Roman potters' kilns of Colchester* (Oxford, 1963).
As well as being the standard work on samian manufacture in Britain, this book is helpful on technical questions.

TECHNICAL

BIMSON, MAVIS, 'The technique of Greek Black and terra sigillata red', *Antiquaries Journal*, xxxvi (1956), p. 200.
Results of experiments in the manufacture of samian carried out in the British Museum Research Laboratory.

LATE RED-GLOSS WARES

HAYES, JOHN, *Late Roman Pottery* (London, 1972).

GENERAL

HARTLEY, B. R., 'Samian ware or terra sigillata', in R. G. Collingwood and I. Richmond, *The Archaeology of Roman Britain* (London, 1969), p. 235.

PLATES

Note:

Unless otherwise stated, all vessels illustrated are in the Department of Prehistoric and Romano-British Antiquities. Numbers prefixed by 'L' (Italian ware) and 'M' (Gaulish ware) refer to Walters's *Catalogue of Roman Pottery* (see Bibliography). Other numbers are departmental registration numbers.

PLATE I

a L.54. Arretine crater, Dr. 11; the stem and foot of the vase are missing (see the Type Table for the form). This vase, decorated with a design showing the Seasons, has an internal stamp of the potter Cn. Ateius. His wares are common in Germany. The date of this piece is Augustan.
Diameter 19 cm.   (*Greek & Roman Antiquities*)   Capua, Italy

b L.56 Arretine jug, decorated with a pattern of leaves and flowers. The stamp of the potter P. Cornelius is incorporated in the decoration, but not visible in the illustration.
Height 15·1 cm., max. diameter, 9·5 cm. (*Greek & Roman Antiquities*)   Italy

PLATE 2

a Arretine cup, form Haltern (Loeschke) 8, stamped by the potter Nicia. Both this form and Hofheim 9, below, continued to be made in the early days of South Gaulish manufacture, but are more typical of Arretine ware. Haltern 8 is seldom found after the Tiberian/early Claudian period.
Diameter 12·9 cm., height 7·6 cm.   Neuss, Germany

b L.169. Arretine cup, form Hofheim (Ritterling) 9, bearing the stamp of Xanthus, a potter working in the factory of Cn. Ateius.
Diameter 10·6 cm., height 5·6 cm.   Provenance unknown, probably Continental

PLATE 3

a Arretine dish, form Dr. 17. The reading of the stamp is uncertain; it is *in planta pedis*, that is, in the shape of a footprint, a feature found only on Arretine and very early South Gaulish wares.

Diameter 15·5 cm., height 3·8 cm.   1929·10–21·3   Basinghall Street, London

b L.138. Late Italian bowl, Dr. 29, stamped by the potter Rasinius Pisanus. This vessel is a copy of South Gaulish ware, and the technique is very poor. It belongs to the second half of the first century A.D.; the form in fact suggests Flavian rather than earlier influence, with its deep rim and sharp angles.

Diameter 29·3 cm., height 13·7 cm.   (*Greek & Roman Antiquities*)   Italy

PLATE 4

a M.5. South Gaulish Dr. 29, stamped LIBNVS. This is an example of the elegant form and restrained decoration of Tiberian South Gaulish ware. The decoration shows direct Arretine influence.
Diameter 20·5 cm., height 7·8 cm. (*Greek & Roman Antiquities*) Eppelsheim, Germany

b South Gaulish Dr. 29 with the stamp of the potter Montanus. The neat, clear moulding and glossy surface of the wares of the Claudian/Neronian period can be seen. The form is somewhat more angular than the earlier bowl shown in 4*a* above.
Diameter 26 cm., height 11 cm.   1915·12–8·53   London

PLATE 5

a M.401. Vase of Dr. 30 decorated in Claudian style. The decoration may be compared with pl. 4*b*.
Diameter 14·8 cm., height 12·1 cm.   44·9–28·2   Sandy, Bedfordshire

b M.610. Dish, Dr. 15/17, with the stamp of the potter Damonus. Claudian.
Diameter 15·2 cm., height 4 cm.   53·5–2·27   Unprovenanced

PLATE 6

a (*left*). A very small South Gaulish cup of form Hofheim 8. This may be compared with the vessel of the same type, only in marbled ware, illustrated on pl. II.
Diameter 6·2 cm., height 3 cm.   53·5–2·37   Eastcheap, London

(*right*). M.776. Cup, Dr. 24/25, with the stamp SALVI. South Gaulish.
Diameter 7·8 cm., height 3·5 cm.   56·7–1·414   London

b M.788. Cup, Dr. 27, stamped by the South Gaulish potter Bassus. The date is probably Neronian. This shape was one of the most common plain forms throughout the first century, and remained popular in the second.
Diameter 11·2 cm., height 5·2 cm.   56·7–1·398   London

PLATE 7

a Dr. 37 bowl of the late Flavian period, stamped by Mercato of South Gaul. The stamp
may be seen in the decoration.
Diameter 24·4 cm., height 12·7 cm.   1931·12–11·1   Great St. Helen's, London

b M.1466. Dr. 37 in the style of the anonymous Trajanic potter of Central Gaul known as
the Potter of the Rosette. The crowded, but lively, design of this freestyle, and the very
good ware and technique, are characteristic of the Trajanic Central Gaulish potters.
The attractive figure–types used by this particular potter were unfortunately not handed
down to be copied by later workers.
Diameter 23·8 cm., height 12·2 cm.   68·8–12·1   Poultry, London

PLATE 8

a M.2365. Central Gaulish vase, Déchelette 72, with applied and barbotine decoration. A vessel as large and elaborate as this is rare; it dates to the Antonine period. The restoration of the rim may not be quite accurate.
Diameter (rim) *c.* 14·5 cm., height 27 cm.   56·7-1·454   Cornhill, London

b M.1463. Freestyle design on a Dr. 37 bowl by the Lezoux potter Paternus, whose stamp may be seen in the decoration. Compare the earlier freestyle by the Potter of the Rosette, (pl. 7*b*). The date of the Paternus bowl is early Antonine.
Diameter 25·5 cm., height 14·2 cm.   94·2–22·1   Wingham, Kent

PLATE 9

A group of unusual decorated forms, Déchelette 67, Déchelette 64, and Knorr 78.

(*left*) M.593. Déch. 67 is a form found in non-Samian pottery, but as a decorated Samian form it is characteristic of the Flavian period in South Gaul. There are also some second-century Central Gaulish examples.
Diameter (max.) 9·8 cm., height 8·1 cm.
Colchester
70·4–2·602

(*centre*) M. 1507. Déch. 64 was made for a relatively short period in the first half of the second century at Lezoux, and appears to have been produced mainly in the work-shops of Libertus and Butrio. The example illustrated is in the style of Libertus. The shape is derived from glass vessels.
Diameter 9·4 cm., height 9 cm.
Colchester
70·4–2·604

(*right*) M.447. Knorr 78 is confined to the Flavian period in South Gaul. It is related to the larger and more elaborate form F 1r. 30
Diameter 11 cm., height 6·9 cm.
Fenchurch Street, London
54·11–30·2

PLATE 10

a (*left*) Dr. 35 in Central Gaulish fabric. Forms 35 and 36 are not normally stamped with a potter's name, except in the case of some from East Gaulish factories.
Diameter 13·2 cm., height 5 cm.   65·12–3·1   King William Street, London

(*right*) M.205. Cup, Dr. 33, in Central Gaulish ware, stamped by the potter Buturrus. This form, like Dr. 27, had a long period of popularity, extending from the mid-first to the third century. It was made at all the major centres of Samian production.
Diameter 10·1 cm., height 4·9 cm.   43·8–12·5   Harpenden, Hertfordshire

b M.1354. Dr. 37 by the firm of Cinnamus, the most important producer at Lezoux in the second century. The large advertisement stamp may clearly be seen. The competent, but somewhat uninspired, scheme of decoration is typical not only of Cinnamus, but of Antonine Central Gaulish Samian in general. Wares of this kind were manufactured and exported in very large quantities.
Diameter 25·8 cm., height 13·6 cm.   66·12–3·81   Unprovenanced

PLATE 11

a A group of unusual plain forms; a small plain jug, an inkpot. and a feeding-bottle. Unusual, specialised forms occur in Samian at all periods, but are somewhat more frequent among East Gaulish wares.

Jug: diameter (max.) 8·5 cm.; height 12·1 cm. 93·6-18·34 Dymchurch, Kent
Inkpot: diameter (base) 7·8 cm., height 5·5 cm. 70·4-2·625 Colchester
Feeding-bottle: diameter (max.) 7·1 cm., height 10·1 cm. 70·4-2·557 Colchester

b Dr. 45, a Samian mortarium form, the interior of which is roughened with grit. This example is in Central Gaulish ware and of Antonine date. The form continued to be made till the fourth century in East Gaul, by which time the neatly-moulded and applied lion's-head spout had been replaced by an amorphous lump faintly resembling a bat's head. The late examples are in very poor, soft ware.

Diameter 24·4 cm., height 11·2 cm. 1921·7-22·3 Billingsgate, London

PLATE 12

a M.2224. Flanged bowl, Dr. 38. This example is stamped by a Rheinzabern potter, Vitalis, but the form was also made in Central Gaul in the Antonine period, and was copied in non-Samian fabrics.

Diameter 15·3 cm., height 7 cm.   65·4–3·3   Broad Street, London

b Dr. 31, East Gaulish ware; the stamp is not legible. This form is the usual plain bowl throughout the second and third centuries. The long graffito inscription on this example is somewhat unusual, though a single name or initial scratched on is fairly common. This piece is probably third century.

Diameter 19·7 cm., height 6·2 cm.   1925·5–2·13   Faversham, Kent

PLATE 13

a M.1429. Dr. 37 made at the East Gaulish centre of Rheinzabern. This bowl is not signed, but is probably by the potter Respectus; the date is late in the second century. The style is closely modelled on Central Gaulish decorated ware, but the execution is inferior. Some other bowls from Rheinzabern were, however, very much less competently made than this one.

Diameter 20·1 cm., height 11·7 cm.   83·10-19·1   London Wall

b M.64. Dr. 37 from the Trier potteries. Bowls from Trier tend to have distinctive designs, inspired very little by the products of other centres. This bowl shows the interesting peculiarity of having an ovolo as the lower border to the decoration as well as the upper. Though the figure-types are crude compared with Central Gaulish examples, the ware, of a rather light orange colour, is very good.

Diameter 24·5 cm., height 14·5 cm.   (*Greek & Roman Antiquities*) Cologne, Germany

PLATE 14

a Dr. 37 with rouletted decoration. This is found from time to time on East Gaulish wares of the second and third centuries, generally on shapes which normally have moulded decoration. The relationship with the later *Rädchensigillata*, with its rows of impressed stamps, is obvious.

Diameter 24·4 cm., height 10 cm.   1931·4-15·20   (*Greek & Roman Antiquities*)
Heddernheim, Germany

b A mould for a bowl of Dr. 37, made by the potter Cerialis of Rheinzabern. Note that the decoration continues up to the rim of the mould; the plain rim of the Samian bowl made in it would have been drawn up above this edge. The small hole in the centre base (not visible in the photograph) and the flange, for ease in handling the mould, are common features. The design may be compared with the Central Gaulish freestyles illustrated on pls. 7*b* and 8*b*.

Diameter 24 cm., height 8 cm.   1939·6-5·1   (*Greek & Roman Antiquities*)
Rheinzabern, Germany

PLATE 15

L.101. A portion of an Arretine mould, and a plaster cast showing the positive impression as it would appear on a vase made in the mould. The stamp of the potter M. Perennius can be seen in the decoration.
Height 11·3 cm.   (*Greek & Roman Antiquities*)   Arezzo, Italy

PLATE 16

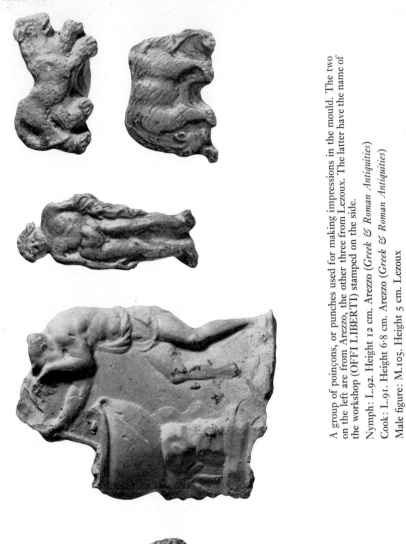

A group of poinçons, or punches used for making impressions in the mould. The two on the left are from Arezzo, the other three from Lezoux. The latter have the name of the workshop (OFFI LIBERTI) stamped on the side.

Nymph: L.92. Height 12 cm. Arezzo (*Greek & Roman Antiquities*)

Cook: L.91. Height 6·8 cm. Arezzo (*Greek & Roman Antiquities*)

Male figure: M.105. Height 5 cm. Lezoux

Panther: M.82. Length 3·8 cm. Lezoux (*Greek & Roman Antiquities*)

Bear: M.83. Length 3·5 cm. Lezoux (*Greek & Roman Antiquities*)